PANORAMA

A HISTORY OF

SHIPS

FROM LOG RAFTS TO LUXURY LINERS

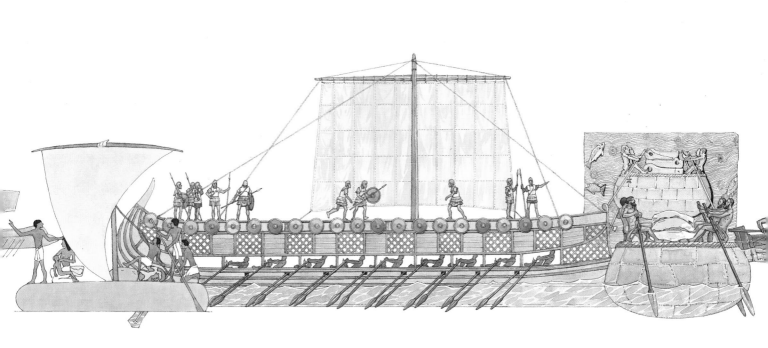

Series designer:	David Salariya
Editor:	Penny Clarke
Artists:	Mark Bergin
	Corinne Burrows
	Ray Burrows
	Nick Hewetson
	John James
	Joe McEwan
	Clyde Pearson
	Lee Peters
	Tony Townsend

Illustrations by:
Mark Bergin 14-15, 22-23; **Corinne and Ray Burrows** 26-27, 28-29, 30-31; **Nick Hewetson** 32-33, 40-41, 42-43; **John James** 10-11, 12-13; **Joe McEwan** 8-9; **Clyde Pearson** 16-17, 18-19; **Lee Peters** 20-21, 24-25; **Tony Townsend** 34-35, 36-37, 38-39.

First published in 1997
by Macdonald Young Books,
an imprint of Wayland Publishers Ltd.
61 Western Road
Hove
East Sussex
BN3 1JD

ISBN 0-7500-1874-7

Author:
Fiona Macdonald studied history at Cambridge University and at the University of East Anglia, where she is a part-time tutor in Medieval History. She has also taught in schools and adult education and is the author of numerous books for children on historical subjects, including *Roman Fort, Viking Town, Medieval Castle, 16th-Century Mosque* and *19th-Century Railway Station* in the **Inside Story** series.

Series designer:
David Salariya was born in Dundee, Scotland, where he studied illustration and printmaking, concentrating on book design in his post-graduate year. He later completed a further post-graduate course in art education at Sussex University. He has illustrated a wide range of books on botanical, historical and mythical subjects. He has designed and created many new series of children's books for publishers in the UK and overseas, including the award-winning **Inside Story** series. He lives in Brighton with his wife, the illustrator Shirley Willis.

© The Salariya Book Co Ltd MCMXCVII

Printed in Hong Kong by

A CIP catalogue record for this book is available from the British Library.

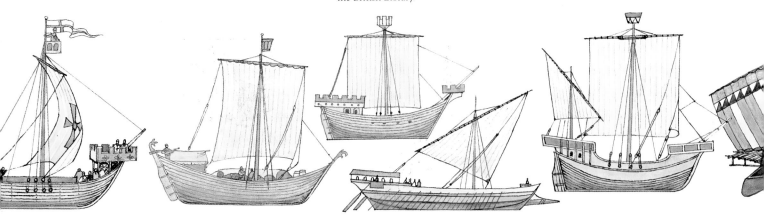

PANORAMA

A HISTORY OF

SHIPS

FROM LOG RAFTS *TO* LUXURY LINERS

Written by
FIONA MACDONALD

Created & Designed by
DAVID SALARIYA

MACDONALD YOUNG BOOKS

Contents

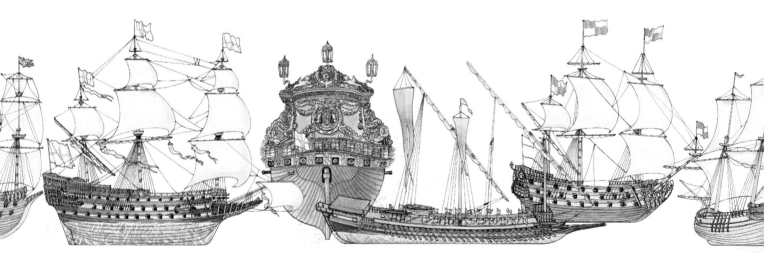

INTRODUCTION

A ship is a machine for carrying loads on water. All ships – from the earliest log raft to the most modern supertanker – have been designed to perform this function. But they are not at all the same. On the following pages, you can see an astonishing variety of water-borne craft from many different centuries and many parts of the world. Each ship that is illustrated has been given a date. Some dates are precise; others can only be approximate.

It is easy to date modern ships; we know exactly when they were first begun, finally completed, or ceremonially launched. But it is far more difficult to date ships that were built a long time ago. There are several reasons for this. Sometimes, there is no written evidence to give us precise information. Sometimes, a ship took ten or twenty years to build, so it might be dated from either the beginning or the end of its time under construction. Sometimes, there have been long-lived series of ships, all copied from one original prototype. And sometimes a ship has had new components added to it, many years after it was first designed.

c3100 BC

c10,000-6000 BC

c3500 BC

c3100 BC

THE FIRST SHIPS

A log is big and heavy, but it is less dense than water, therefore it floats. It can also provide extra buoyancy for people holding on to it.

BOATS helped hunters exploit new hunting grounds. They provided a mobile base which could be rowed or paddled to a site close to a likely source of prey, for example, an animals' drinking hole or a water-birds' breeding site.

N_{o one} knows exactly when the first ships were built. People have travelled by water for thousands of years – long before the first written records. Most archaeologists think that the first 'ship' was not made at all – it just happened by chance. Perhaps someone saw a log that had fallen into a river, sat on it, and paddled with their hands. They discovered that even with extra weight on top, the log would still float, and that by moving one hand faster than the other, they could steer it in the direction they wanted to go.

After a breakthrough like this, the next step (probably around 10,000 BC) was to tie several logs together to form a raft. Where local timber was suitable, boatbuilders might also hollow out a tree-trunk to make a simple canoe. Where there was no suitable timber, rafts might be made from animal skins, reeds or woven twigs.

TREE-TRUNKS could be hollowed to make 'dugout' boats in two different ways: by soaking the wood in water until it softened and then scraping out the core, or by making fires in small holes along one side and then chipping out the burned wood.

THE SIDES of the dugout boat were smoothed and trimmed, and the ends were pointed or rounded to make the bow and the stern.

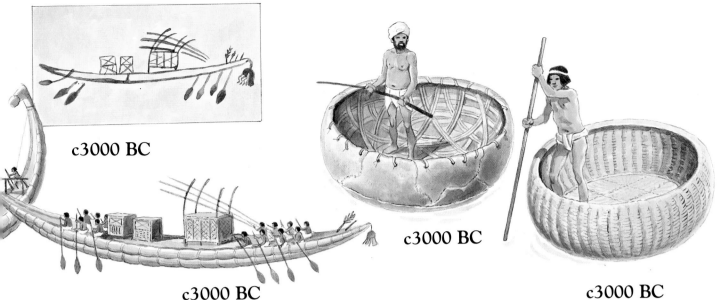

c3000 BC

c3000 BC

c3000 BC

c3000 BC

SHIPS AND BOATS
Today, we use the word 'ship' to mean a large vessel, and the word 'boat' to mean a small one. There is no precise dividing line between the two. In the past, the word 'ship' had a technical meaning. It meant a vessel with three or more masts, all carrying square sails. The word 'boat' was used to describe a much smaller craft, which might be carried on board a ship and used to ferry sailors and passengers ashore.

c10,000-6000 BC Raft, made by tying logs together to create a platform where one or more people could stand. Rafts like this were pushed through the water with hands or poles.

c3500 BC Raft made of inflated animal skins. After the meat and bones had been removed, an animal skin could be sewn up and filled with air (by blowing down the neck) to provide bouyancy.

c3100 BC Boat made of bundles of reeds, with a rectangular sail, painted on a pottery vase from Egypt.

c3100 BC Modern reconstruction of the same boat.

c3000 BC Painting of a reed boat from Egypt, used to ferry cargo along the River Nile. It was propelled by paddles, and steered by a single oar at the stern (back). It had a small cabin on board. Cargo was stowed on the open deck.

c3000 BC Modern reconstruction of the same boat.

c3000 BC Buffalo boat or paracil, made of strips of bamboo covered with animal hide, from southern India. Similar boats were made in Europe and North America, and are still used in India.

c3000 BC Quffa, or basket boat from Mesopotamia (present-day Iraq). It is made of tightly-woven reeds. Ancient, traditional boat designs like this are still used in Iraq.

IN COUNTRIES where there were few trees and not much timber, boats were made of bundles of reeds, tied together with rope.

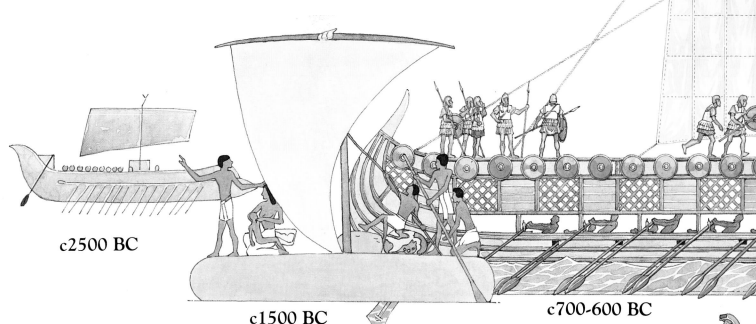

c2500 BC

c1500 BC

c700-600 BC

Oars and Sails

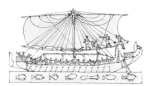

Egyptian seagoing ships, c1500 BC. Ships like this made journeys down the Red Sea and the East African coast to Punt (present-day Somalia), a distance of over 2000 kilometres.

It is very hard work using your hands to push a boat through the water. So, soon after the earliest rafts and canoes were built, simple paddles were invented, too. They acted like enormous hands, scooping the water aside.

There were two different types of paddle: single (with one wide blade at the end of a short pole) or double (with a blade at both ends). Double paddles were easier to use. You could dip each blade in the water alternately, rather than lifting the whole paddle from side to side of your raft or canoe.

Some time later, oars (one blade at one end of a long pole) were developed. They could be used to row a boat. Rowing was easier than paddling – oars do not have to be lifted as high out of the water as a paddle – so boats could be bigger, to travel faster and carry larger loads. When fixed at the stern of a boat, an oar could be used to steer.

By around 5000 BC, boats also began to be built with sails. People observed how powerful the wind was, and one clever boatbuilder found a way of 'trapping' this wind-power by using a large sail. Originally, sails were made of skins, leaves or matting, but soon thick cloth was used.

EGYPTIAN trade routes. Wheat from Egypt was exported to many Mediterranean lands. Egypt imported timber, precious stones and dyestuffs from present-day Lebanon.

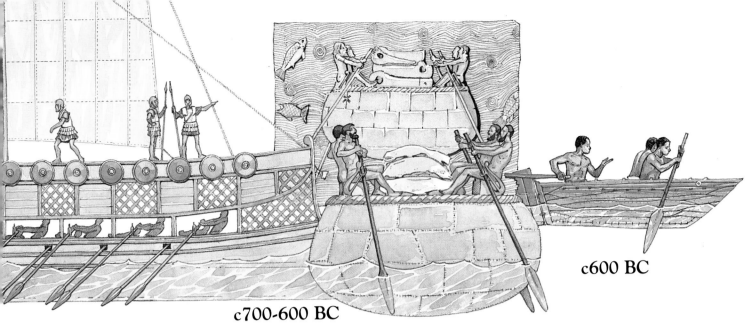

c700-600 BC

c600 BC

MODELS of two different types of Egyptian boat found in tombs, c2000 BC.

EGYPTIAN cargo ship, c2600 BC. It had a big single sail, but could also be rowed with oars. It was steered by one large oar at the stern. Ships like this sailed along the River Nile.

Stone carving from Medinet Habu, Egypt, c1176 BC, showing a battle at sea.

EGYPTIAN royal barge, built for Pharaoh Khufu, c2800 BC, from precious cedarwood, brought from Lebanon. Almost 43 metres long, it was rowed.

c2500 BC Seagoing Hittite ship from the southern shores of the Black Sea in Anatolia (present-day Turkey). Made of wooden planks, it is long and slim, propelled by oars and a sail. It was used to carry soldiers to war.

c1500 BC Rafts with big square sails and skin floats added for extra bouyancy. Carved on the tomb of Egyptian pharaoh Amenophis II, these rafts were part of a trading expedition down the Red Sea to Punt (present-day Somalia). Rafts like these were used to transport valuable cargoes such as ivory, incense and slaves.

c700-600 BC Fighting ship built by the Phoenicians (from present-day Lebanon) to guard their convoys of merchant ships. It was powered by oars and a sail. For defence, rows of soldiers' shields were hung around the outer edge of the deck.

c700-600 BC River-boat made of bundles of reeds or twisted branches, covered with skins. It was pictured on the tomb of Assyrian emperor Sennacherib in the city of Ninevah (in present-day Iraq). A reconstruction of the boat is drawn in front.

c600 BC A mtepe, a boat made of planks of wood sewn together with strong twine, from East Africa (the region of present-day Tanzania). Used to sail in river estuaries and along the coast. These boats were first recorded during the 6th century BC, but may have been invented many hundreds of years before.

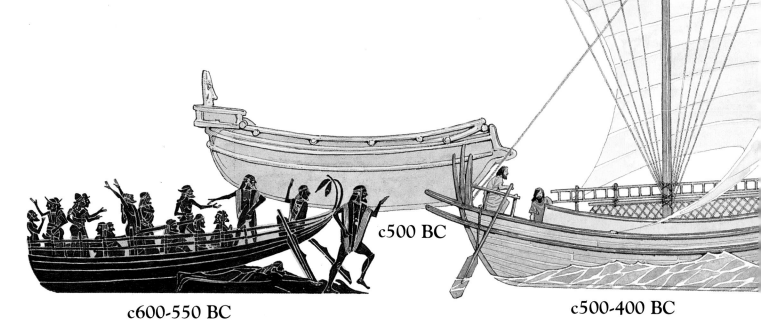

c600-550 BC

c500 BC

c500-400 BC

Designing the Hull

Ram from the front of a Greek warship, used to ram and hole enemy ships below the water-line so they would sink.

Ships hollowed-out of logs could only be as long as the tree-trunk they were made from. As early as 2500 BC, shipbuilders and carpenters had found a way of using sawn or shaped planks of wood to construct purpose-built hulls (the part of the boat that is in the water) for their boats. But, by around 600 BC, ancient Greek and Roman shipbuilders were building different types of ship for different purposes.

If a ship was going to carry cargo such as wine or grain it had a wide, rounded hull. Speed was not important, so its main power came from the wind, caught in a big square sail. If the wind dropped and the ship was becalmed (unable to move), then its cargo would have to wait. Cargo ships had room for a few rowers to get them safely into harbour or through narrow channels, but not enough to row long distances.

If the new boat was going to be a warship, then it needed to be fast. A slim, streamlined hull was best, and there had to be room for plenty of oarsmen in case the wind dropped. No soldier wanted to be trapped in enemy waters and unable to get away. Warships also had a lethal 'ram' (a sharp point below the water-line) and a strong, flat deck from which soldiers could leap aboard enemy ships.

VERY FEW remains have been found of complete Greek ships, so most of what we know about them comes from vase-paintings. This vase was made in Athens in the 6th century BC.

hoplites (foot-soldiers)

oculus keeps 'evil eye' away

oars

ram

500-400 BC

200-100 BC

c500-300 BC

100 BC   **AD 100**

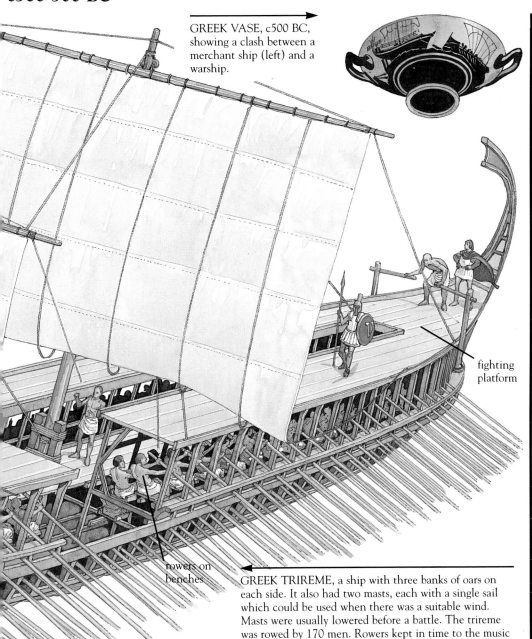

GREEK VASE, c500 BC, showing a clash between a merchant ship (left) and a warship.

fighting platform

rowers on benches

GREEK TRIREME, a ship with three banks of oars on each side. It also had two masts, each with a single sail which could be used when there was a suitable wind. Masts were usually lowered before a battle. The trireme was rowed by 170 men. Rowers kept in time to the music of flutes. Triremes carried a crew of hoplites, well-armed soldiers, ready to board enemy ships and fight.

c600-550 BC Greek long ship, used to carry soldiers to battles fought between rival city-states on the Greek islands and around the coast.

c500 BC Merchant ship from Cyprus, built with a deep, rounded hull to provide room for lots of cargo.

c500-400 BC Greek merchant ship. Like the Cypriot vessel, it has a massive round hull to store cargo. Sailors climbed aboard up a ladder, stored neatly at the stern. It was powered by sail, and steered by a single oar.

c500-400 BC Greek triakontor (ship with 30 oars). In contrast with the merchant ship (above), it is long and sleek, designed to travel swiftly through the water.

c500-300 BC War-canoe from Hjortsprung, Denmark, made of overlapping wooden planks sewn together with rope.

200-100 BC A masula, a boat built for use in the high surf off the Coromandel coast of south-east India. It is made of broad, thin planks, sewn together by rope twisted from coconut fibre (called coir).

100 BC Roman warship with three banks (tiers) of oars. Ships like this were slow and heavy compared with the lightweight Greek triakontor above.

AD 100 Round-hulled Roman merchant ship. It had two oars at the stern for steering. Crews and cargo came on board via the corvus (gangplank), a Roman invention.

c500

c600-700

827

Vikings and Nearby Lands

Viking warships were often decorated with a wood-carving of a fierce dragon's head at the prow.

For Greek and Roman armies, war at sea had been much less important than battles on land. But for the Vikings, pirates and explorers who flourished in northern Europe between around AD 800-1100, ships were a vitally important weapon. Viking sea-raiders swooped down on coastal villages, monasteries and farms, bringing death and destruction to the inhabitants and returning home with rich treasures.

Viking long ships were made of overlapping planks of wood to give strength and flexibility to withstand rough seas, and with room for sixteen oars each side. The oar-holes were covered with wooden disks, to keep the water out when the ship was sailing. The long ships were also shallow. There were no seats or decks; sailors rowed sitting on their sea-chests, and any cargo was covered by waterproof oiled cloths. There was a big square sail made of fabric strengthened with strips of leather, and a steering oar at the stern. The mast was held firm by ropes and a large block of wood called the mast-step.

The Vikings had trading vessels, too. Knorrs were purpose-built cargo ships, but other slow, wide-bodied craft were used to ferry goods around the coast of Scandinavia.

VIKING shipbuilders at work. The planks used in many ships were only 2.5 centimetres thick. The Vikings had no saws, so they cut and shaped the wood with axes, adzes and moulding irons (an early plane).

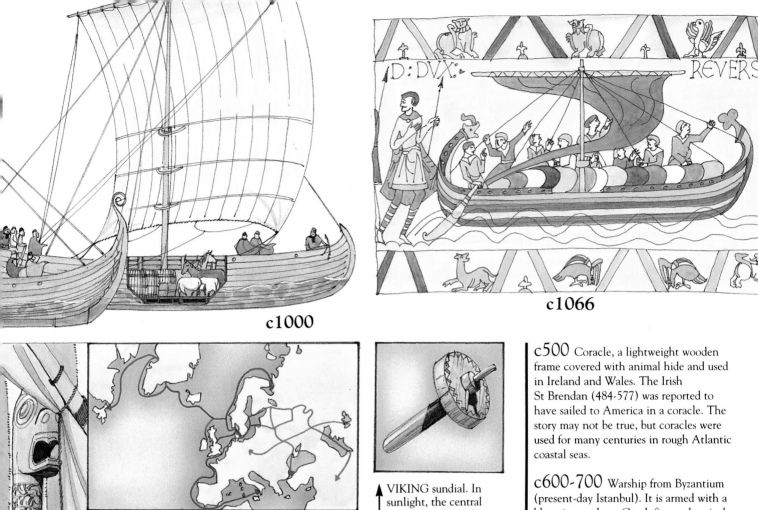

c1000

c1066

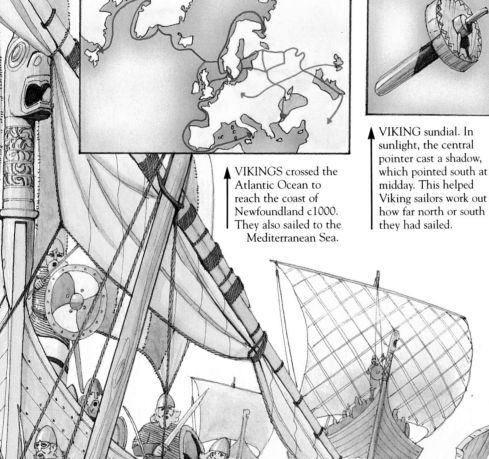

VIKING sundial. In sunlight, the central pointer cast a shadow, which pointed south at midday. This helped Viking sailors work out how far north or south they had sailed.

VIKINGS crossed the Atlantic Ocean to reach the coast of Newfoundland c1000. They also sailed to the Mediterranean Sea.

VIKINGS attack a Muslim boat in the Mediterranean.

c500 Coracle, a lightweight wooden frame covered with animal hide and used in Ireland and Wales. The Irish St Brendan (484-577) was reported to have sailed to America in a coracle. The story may not be true, but coracles were used for many centuries in rough Atlantic coastal seas.

c600-700 Warship from Byzantium (present-day Istanbul). It is armed with a blowpipe to shoot Greek fire, a chemical mixture that burned with a very hot flame which could not be put out by water. Because it was oil-based and floated on the surface of the sea, Greek fire could cause terrible damage to enemy ships.

827 The Oseberg ship, a royal Viking ship used for short trips around the coast. It is built of wooden planks in lapstrake or clinker style: each plank overlaps the one below. It is 20 metres long and about 6 metres wide.

c1000 Viking cargo ship (capacity 24 tonnes) found at Skuldelev, Denmark. It is 16.3 metres long and wide-bodied. It was designed for long sea voyages; most of its power came from a huge sail 100 metres square. Its six-man crew was equipped with oars, but these would have been used only in emergencies or when approaching land.

c1066 Picture of the ship sailed by King Harold, the last Saxon king of England, from the Bayeux Tapestry (c1080). Harold's ship was very similar to Norman and Viking warships.

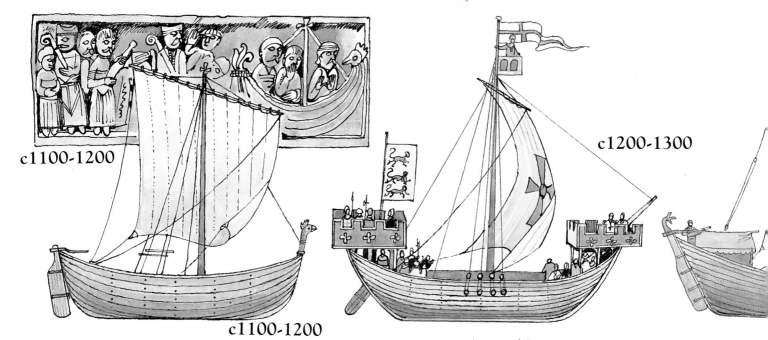

c1100-1200

c1200-1300

c1100-1200

EUROPE: THE MIDDLE AGES

In medieval times (c1000-1500), important documents had seals fixed to them to show they were genuine. This seal belonged to the port of Winchelsea, in southern England. It shows a cog.

Viking ships

were so well designed that similar ships were used in many European lands for hundreds of years. But, by around 1200, changes were beginning to be made. Fighting platforms called castles were added to the bow (front) and the stern of warships, and a circular platform called a fighting top was built at the top of the main mast. It was an ideal lookout point, and a place where archers could stand to shoot arrows at enemy ships below. Gradually the Viking steering oar was replaced by a rudder (an upright paddle) mounted at the stern.

Ships were becoming bigger, too, so there was more room within the hull to build one or two tiers of decks. Warships remained longer and slimmer than cargo ships; the typical medieval cargo ship was called a hulc or, by 1350, a cog.

Until around 1400, most European ships had only one mast. In the north sails were square, as Viking sails had been. In southern Europe, triangular or lateen sails, were used. Around 1400, northern shipbuilders began to copy southern building styles. Ships' timbers were now joined edge to edge, carvel style, rather than overlapping.

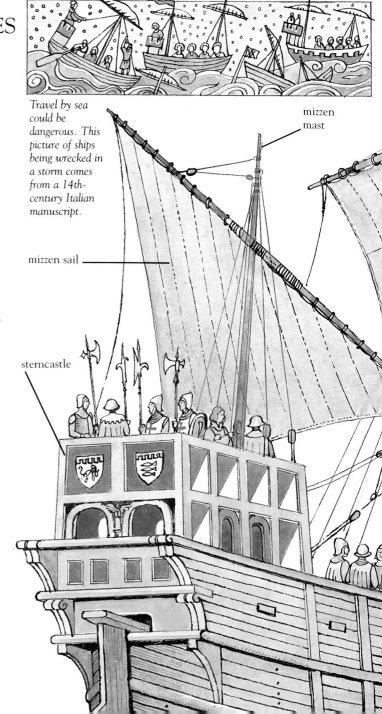

Travel by sea could be dangerous. This picture of ships being wrecked in a storm comes from a 14th-century Italian manuscript.

mizzen mast

mizzen sail

sterncastle

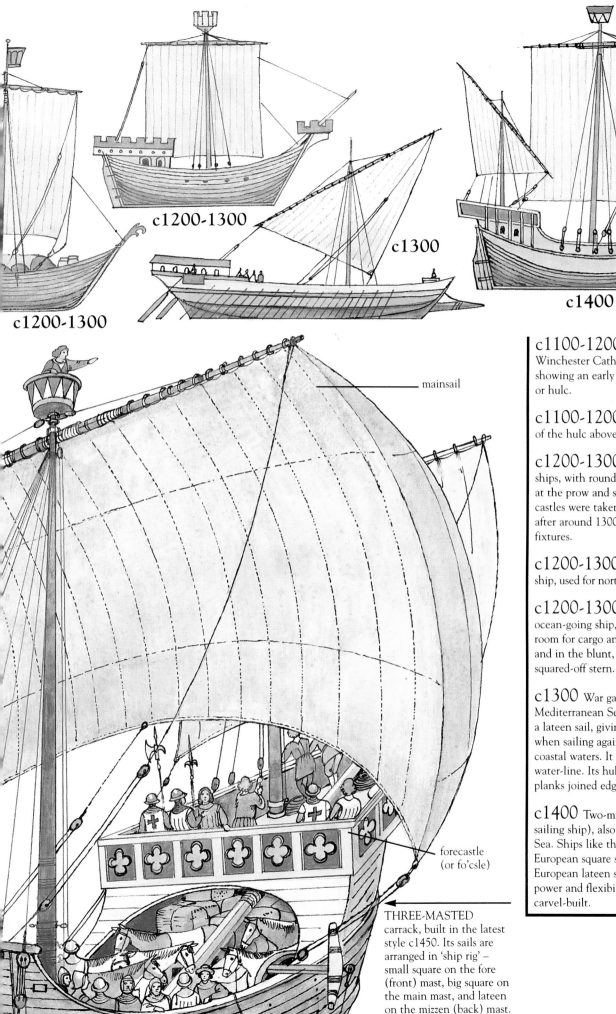

c1200-1300

c1200-1300

c1300

c1400

mainsail

forecastle
(or fo'csle)

THREE-MASTED
carrack, built in the latest
style c1450. Its sails are
arranged in 'ship rig' –
small square on the fore
(front) mast, big square on
the main mast, and lateen
on the mizzen (back) mast.

c1100-1200 Carved stone font,
Winchester Cathedral, southern England,
showing an early medieval trading ship,
or hulc.

c1100-1200 Modern reconstruction
of the hulc above.

c1200-1300 English troop-carrying
ships, with rounded hulls and castles built
at the prow and stern. At first these
castles were taken down in peacetime, but
after around 1300 they became permanent
fixtures.

c1200-1300 Small round-hulled
ship, used for north-European coastal trade.

c1200-1300 English clinker-built
ocean-going ship, called a cog. It has
room for cargo and passengers in the hull
and in the blunt, rounded prow and
squared-off stern.

c1300 War galley from the
Mediterranean Sea. It has rows of oars and
a lateen sail, giving good manoeuvrability
when sailing against the wind in shallow
coastal waters. It also has a ram below the
water-line. Its hull is carvel-built, made of
planks joined edge to edge.

c1400 Two-masted carrack (large
sailing ship), also from the Mediterranean
Sea. Ships like this combined northern
European square sails with southern
European lateen sails to give maximum
power and flexibility. Its hull was
carvel-built.

17

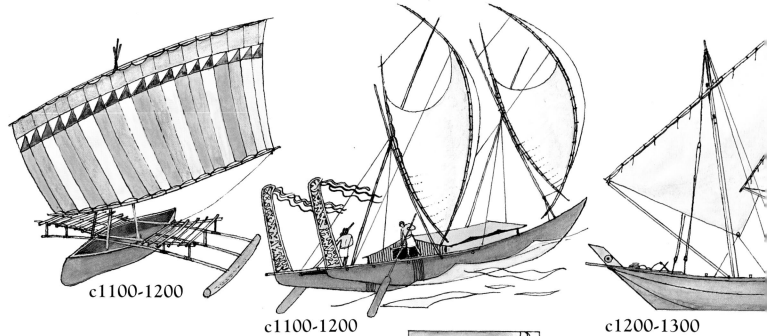

c1100-1200

c1100-1200

c1200-1300

ASIA AND THE PACIFIC

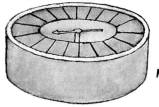

Chinese compass. It used a magnetized metal pointer to indicate north. Compasses like these were unknown in the West until after 1400.

Nanking
Chittagong

T he most skilful sailors of the medieval era lived in Asia and the Far East. Muslim sailors from Arabia, East Africa and the Indian subcontinent sailed two-masted dhows on regular trading voyages across the Indian Ocean and to the rich Spice Islands of Indonesia. A few Muslim explorers may even have reached China, a journey of almost 10,000 kilometres. Muslim sailors were expert navigators, plotting their courses by the sun and brilliant tropical stars. They also invented devices like the kamal and the astrolabe to help their navigation.

Medieval Chinese sailed flat-bottomed junks on trading voyages all round the South China Sea, and may even have sighted the north coast of Australia. Chinese sailors invented the compass, the rudder and watertight compartments to help stop ships sinking – all great advances in technology. Pacific Ocean islanders sailed big double-hulled canoes, from Hawaii to New Zealand steering by the stars – there are no landmarks on the ocean.

sails made of reed matting

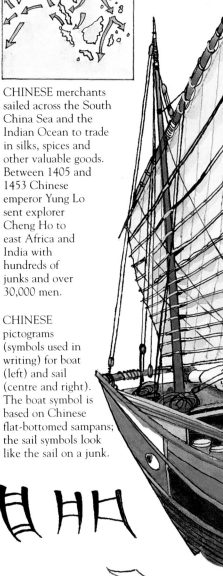

CHINESE merchants sailed across the South China Sea and the Indian Ocean to trade in silks, spices and other valuable goods. Between 1405 and 1453 Chinese emperor Yung Lo sent explorer Cheng Ho to east Africa and India with hundreds of junks and over 30,000 men.

CHINESE pictograms (symbols used in writing) for boat (left) and sail (centre and right). The boat symbol is based on Chinese flat-bottomed sampans; the sail symbols look like the sail on a junk.

c1237

c1450

c1237

c1377

AN ASTROLABE, a navigation instrument invented by Muslim sailors. It was used to measure the height of the sun above the horizon at midday, or the position of the Pole Star at midnight. The further a ship was from the equator, the lower the sun (or the Pole Star) seemed to be. This helped sailors out of sight of land work out their position north or south.

MEDIEVAL Chinese trading junk

MAP OF THE WORLD, drawn by a medieval Muslim scholar. It shows Africa, Arabia, India and the Indian Ocean, as well as Spain and the Mediterranean Sea.

SAILORS from islands in the Pacific Ocean made maps out of shells and sticks. The shells represented islands; the sticks showed ocean currents and winds.

c1100-1200 Log raft, with sail, from the Tuatmotu Islands in the Pacific Ocean. Some log rafts could be up to 30 metres long.

c1100-1200 Polynesian Wa'a-kaulua canoe. It has twin hulls, and was designed for long-distance ocean voyages. Migrants from Hawaii sailed in canoes like these to explore the Pacific Ocean and found settlements in New Zealand.

c1200-1300 Arab dhow, or seagoing cargo vessel. It has two masts and a lateen sail. The hull was made of planks stitched together with coir. Smaller, simpler dhows probably originated in the 9th century AD.

c1237 Arab sewn plank-boat, recorded in a manuscript written by the famous 13th-century scholar, al-Hariri. Boats like these were made of palm-trunks, or of teak imported from India. They sailed in the Persian Gulf and the Indian Ocean, and may have reached China.

c1237 Modern reconstruction of the Arab sewn-plank boat above.

c1377 Chinese sampan or river-boat. This example dates from the 14th century, but similar shallow, flat-bottomed boats had probably been used on Chinese rivers for hundreds of years.

c1450 Japanese plank-boat, called a yamato-gata. Planks for the hull were joined edge to edge. There was no inner frame.

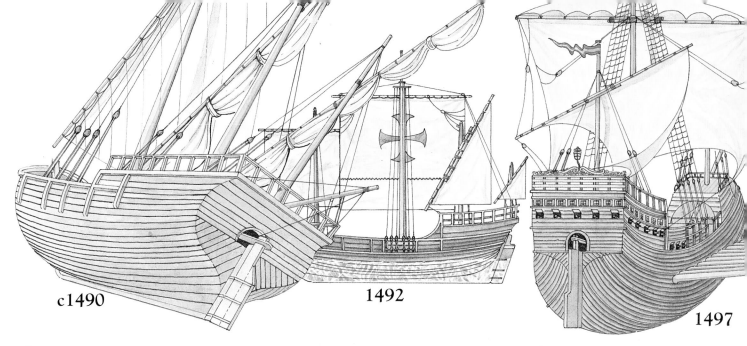

c1490   1492   1497

EXPLORING THE WORLD

Fanciful drawing of a warship, from an Italian book printed in 1472. No such ship was ever built.

Throughout the 15th century, navigators tried to find a new way to travel to the rich lands of the East. They hoped a sea-route would be quicker than the existing overland journey, which often took several years. It would be more profitable, too, since ships could carry larger quantities of precious silks and spices than horses and carts.

Portuguese sailors pioneered an eastwards route, along the west coast of Africa, round the Cape of Good Hope and across the Indian Ocean. They were finally successful: Vasco da Gama arrived in India in 1498.

The Portuguese sailed in ships called caravels. These were small (usually less than 30 metres long), fast and good for exploring shallow waters around unknown coasts. They could be converted for ocean sailing by adding big square sails to catch more wind. Later, once the Indian Ocean sea-routes were better-known, explorers sailed in huge, wide-bodied carracks. These were slow and cumbersome, but they could carry far more valuable cargoes from the east.

Other explorers, Christopher Columbus in 1492, then Ferdinand Magellan and Juan Sebastian del Cano in 1519-1522, tried to find a westward route to the east. They were all financed by Spain, Portugal's great rival.

15TH-CENTURY compass (left). Traverse-board (right) used by sailors to record their course. Every half hour a peg was placed in one of the holes in the compass design to show the ship's direction.

COLUMBUS made four journeys across the Atlantic between 1492-1500. On each trip he explored a little more of the Caribbean and Central American coast.

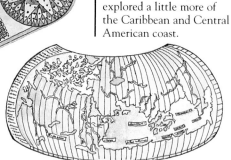

LATE 15th-century map, showing the world as many geographers believed it to be. America is not shown, because no Europeans or Asians knew it was there.

VIEW of the Italian port of Genoa, 1486, showing ships anchored in its deep harbour.

c1500

c1540

square sail

lateen
sail

THE *Santa Maria*,
Columbus's flagship
and one of the three ships
he took on his pioneering
voyage to America in
1492. The *Santa Maria* was
a typical small caravel, re-
rigged with square sails for
the ocean voyage. It was
wrecked off Haiti and
abandoned there.

rigging

stern deck

c1490 Fishing-boat from the
Mediterranean. Vessels like this had a
deck covering cargo space in the hull, a
square stern and one, two or three masts
for the lateen sails.

1492 The *Niña*, one of the three ships
Columbus sailed in on his epic voyage to
America. Originally, the *Niña* had lateen
sails. But Columbus changed them to
north-European square sails. This helped
the *Niña* sail better in the strong, easterly
Atlantic winds. *Niña* was a caravel – a
small, fast, shallow, three-masted ship,
very suitable for voyages of exploration.

1497 Ship sailed by Portuguese
explorer Vasco da Gama on his pioneering
voyage around the Cape of Good Hope
and across the Indian Ocean to reach
India. He was the first European sailor to
do this.

c1500 Mediterranean galleass, a
warship powered by oars as well as by a
sail. Galleasses were very useful in
sheltered seas, or for manoeuvring in
shallow waters, but they were less
seaworthy in strong winds or high seas.

c1540 The *Galie Subtile*, a magnificent
ceremonial warship with oars. Built for
King Henry VIII of England (reigned
1509-1547) by Italian shipwrights to
Mediterranean designs.

anchor

hold

rudder

21

1545

c1550

CANNON FIRE

Queen Elizabeth I of England (ruled 1558-1603) supported Sir Francis Drake, the second captain to sail his ship right round the world.

Ever since Greek and Roman times, sea battles had been fought in one of two ways. Ships either tried to ram and sink one another, or else an attacking ship sailed close alongside its target while the crew threw Greek fire or shot arrows at their enemies. Soldiers also tried to board enemy ships to fight on deck.

Since the 15th century, cannon had been used by armies on land to smash great holes in castle walls. By the 1540s, warships and battle tactics were being designed to make use of these new weapons. Ships fighting at sea tried to keep a safe distance while pounding their enemies with cannon fire. Now warships needed to be stronger, to support the heavy cannon and to withstand the shock when they were fired. This extra weight meant they had to carry larger areas of sail.

Rulers like King Henry VIII of England ordered new ships to be built to heavy carrack designs. Then holes, called gun-ports, were cut into their hulls, so the cannon could be fired through them. Sometimes, this led to disaster: in 1545 the *Mary Rose* capsized and sank. But by the end of the 16th century, many huge but seaworthy gunships had been built.

Loading a cannon with gunpowder and a cannon-ball, ready to fire.

ENGLISH longbowman, early 16th century. For centuries, shipboard archers had fired arrows at enemies on neighbouring vessels. But they were being replaced by cannon (big, wheel-mounted guns).

royal arms of England

THE GALLEON *Ark Royal*, built 1587, flagship of the English navy at the time of the Armada. It has a low castle at the stern, giving better stability than earlier top-heavy ships like the *Mary Rose*. The hull is also less 'sheer' – that is, it is straight, rather than curved in a half-moon shape. The gun-ports are placed below decks, but, for safety, well above the water-line.

bow

22

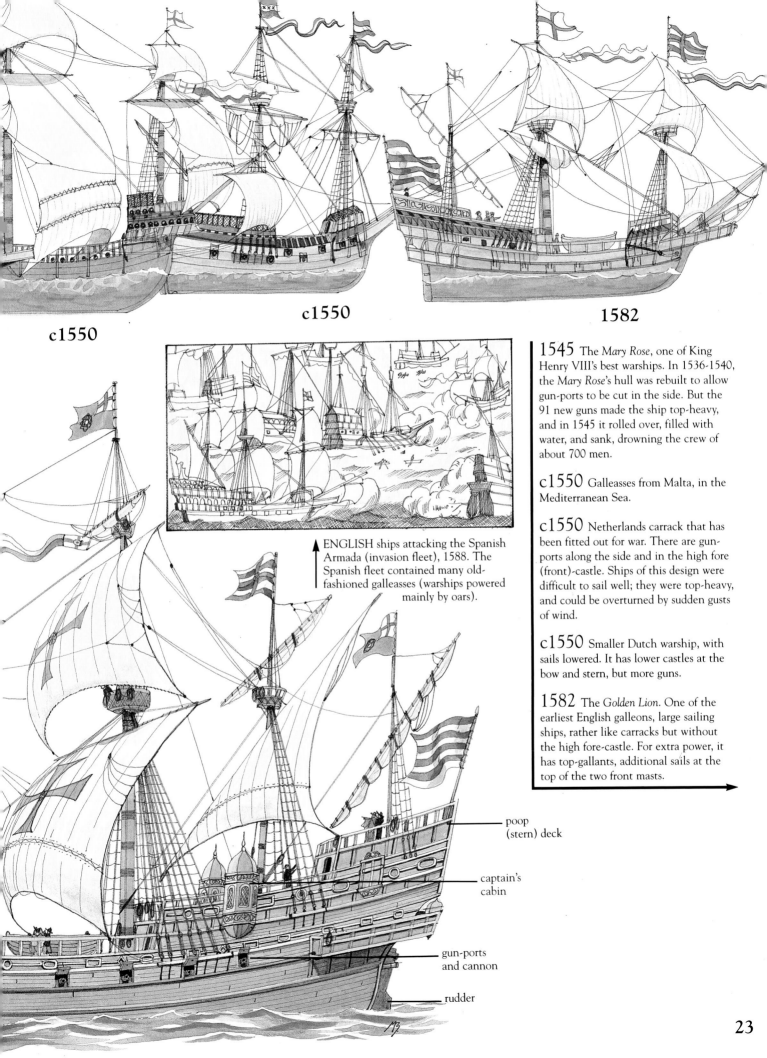

c1550

c1550

1582

c1550

ENGLISH ships attacking the Spanish Armada (invasion fleet), 1588. The Spanish fleet contained many old-fashioned galleasses (warships powered mainly by oars).

1545 The *Mary Rose*, one of King Henry VIII's best warships. In 1536-1540, the *Mary Rose*'s hull was rebuilt to allow gun-ports to be cut in the side. But the 91 new guns made the ship top-heavy, and in 1545 it rolled over, filled with water, and sank, drowning the crew of about 700 men.

c1550 Galleasses from Malta, in the Mediterranean Sea.

c1550 Netherlands carrack that has been fitted out for war. There are gun-ports along the side and in the high fore (front)-castle. Ships of this design were difficult to sail well; they were top-heavy, and could be overturned by sudden gusts of wind.

c1550 Smaller Dutch warship, with sails lowered. It has lower castles at the bow and stern, but more guns.

1582 The *Golden Lion*. One of the earliest English galleons, large sailing ships, rather like carracks but without the high fore-castle. For extra power, it has top-gallants, additional sails at the top of the two front masts.

poop
(stern) deck

captain's
cabin

gun-ports
and cannon

rudder

1628

1637

1665

EUROPE AND AMERICA

Submarine designed by Cornelius Drebbel in 1620. It was propelled by oars sticking out of the hull through leather flaps.

After Columbus's epic voyage, Europeans began to settle in America and shipowners began to establish new transatlantic sea routes between Europe and America. Huge Spanish galleons, loaded with silver and other treasures from Mexico and Peru, sailed back to Spain. These Spanish treasure convoys were guarded by massive gunships, almost twice as big as the galleons although similar in design.

By the end of the 16th century sail design had changed. Now there were three sets of sails on each mast, rather than one or two enormous ones. This was an important safety feature, because the small top sails could be lowered quickly in a storm, so making the ship less top-heavy.

In contrast to the huge treasure-ships and their escorts, the tiny (29-metre) *Mayflower* was an ordinary merchant ship, of the type that regularly made the Atlantic crossing. The *Mayflower* took the Puritans, a group seeking religious freedom, from England to start a new life in America. With over 100 people on board the voyage was cramped and miserable, but they survived and prospered in the New World.

SHIPS were still built of wood. They were based on a massive wooden backbone, called a keel.

mizzen sail (lateen-shaped)

rear hold

THE *Mayflower* was about 29 metres long and 8 metres wide. It had a crew of about 25.

main hold

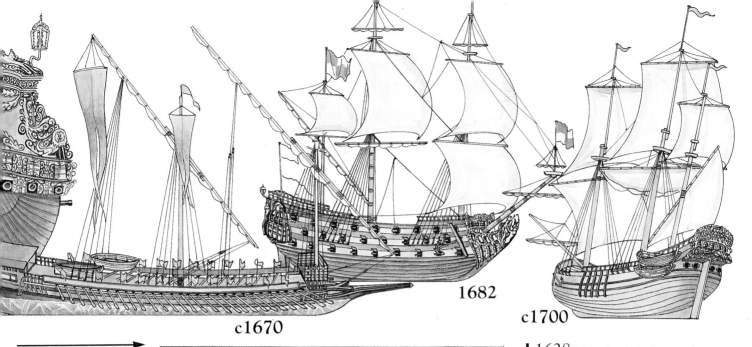

1682

c1670

c1700

WATER PAGEANT on the River Thames in London in 1662 to welcome Catherine of Braganza, bride of King Charles II, when she arrived by ship from her home in Portugal.

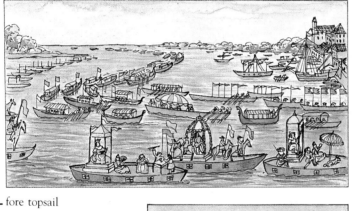

fore topsail

crow's nest (lookout point)

fore sail

1628 The splendidly-decorated Swedish warship *Vasa*. Like the *Mary Rose* (page 22) the guns above the water-line made this ship top-heavy. It was also very narrow for its height. It sank in Stockholm harbour on its maiden voyage.

1637 The *Sovereign of the Seas*, a 100-gun warship, and the first British man-of-war to have its guns arranged on three decks. It was accidentally destroyed by fire in 1696.

1665 Dutch warship, with three masts, a single gun-deck and a magnificently decorated stern.

c1670 French war-galley, built to sail in the Mediterranean. It has 60 oars and two lateen sails.

1682 The *Britannia*, a British warship with 100 guns.

c1700 Dutch whaler, typical of the merchant ships which sailed each year to catch whales in the icy Arctic seas. Whalers' bows were strengthened to help them sail among ice floes. Sometimes they got trapped by the ice, and had to spend all winter away from home.

AS WELL AS the passengers and crew, the *Mayflower* carried everything they needed for their new life.

A GONDOLA, a large, elegant canoe from the Italian city of Venice, c1750. Venice is built on the water; it has lakes and canals instead of streets.

c1550

c1590

1600

New Ships, New Lands

Native American birchbark canoes. Drawn by the 17th-century French traveller Samuel de Champlain, who explored north-eastern America.

Until the Spanish and Portuguese voyages of exploration in the late 15th century, most European sailors had never seen non-European ships. A few bold adventurers, like Marco Polo who travelled overland to China in the 13th century, came home with admiring descriptions of Chinese junks. And some Mediterranean traders might have heard about African and Indian shipping from the travelling Muslim merchants with whom they traded. But accurate, detailed knowledge about the amazing variety of different ships to be seen in different parts of the world did not reach European scholars and sailors until the late 16th and early 17th centuries. Then, it was eagerly reported in illustrated books, produced on printing presses which were still a new and exciting invention. Travellers' tales and scientific reports, like those published in 1601 by the Dutch writer de Bry, proved immensely popular.

NATIVE AMERICAN canoes were strong but light. They could be carried overland (this was called 'portage') where rivers were blocked by rapids or waterfalls.

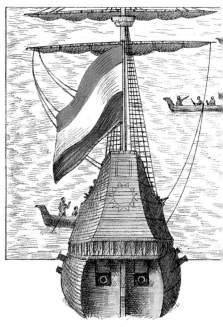

LARGE Dutch galleons anchored off the remote Pacific island of Guam, and surrounded by a variety of local craft.

CANOE of eucalyptus tree bark, used by the aboriginal peoples of Australia for fishing.

A PAGE from the journal kept by Dutch explorer Abel Tasman (1603-1659), showing Pacific islanders paddling a large double-hulled canoe.

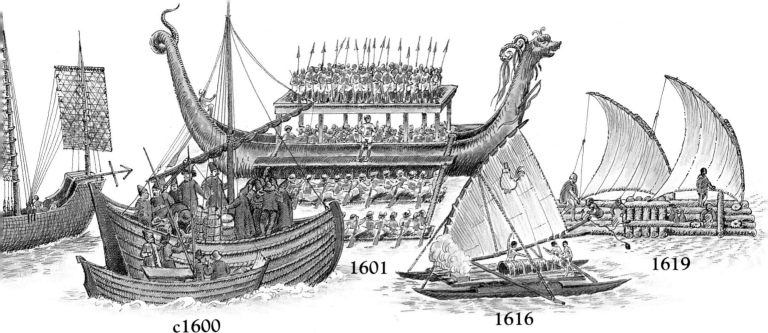

1601

1619

c1600

1616

CANOE made by the Algonkian people of southern Canada, using thin strips of bark, lashed to a rigid wooden frame.

c1550 Raft made from reeds, sailed on Lake Titicaca, high in the Andes mountains of South America where no trees grow. The single sail is also made of reeds.

c1590 Canoe with two outriggers and a small sail, from Banda in the Molucca Islands (in present-day Indonesia). The outriggers increased the canoe's stability.

1600 Japanese sailing vessel off the coast of the Philippines. It has sails made of matting.

c1600 Two boats from Lapland, seen by the Dutch explorer, Wilhelm Barents, in the seas off northern Russia.

1601 A kora kora, a large log boat with outriggers (seats for men with paddles) on either side, from Banda in the Molucca Islands. It had a large, central cabin, tall, carved prow and stern, and a single steering oar.

1616 Paired boat (two hulls lashed together, with a gap in between) from Tonga, in the Pacific. Linking small, narrow hulls like this gave the finished boat more stability in the high waves of the Pacific.

1619 Seagoing log raft from Peru. It has twin triangular sails and is fitted with guares, adjustable keel-boards which helped the raft maintain balance and made steering easier.

THIS SCENE was pictured by the Dutch explorer de Bry in a book published in 1619. Most of the local boats are canoes. Some have sails, others are propelled by paddles.

1701

1710-1722

1728

INTERNATIONAL TRADE

A whipping with the 'cat of nine tails' was feared by even the toughest of seamen.

Ships have always been used for international trade. Little boats have been used for fishing and as local ferries, too. But during the 17th and 18th centuries, European fishing fleets regularly made much longer journeys across the ocean to the teeming seas around Newfoundland, off the Canadian coast. There were now also regular long-distance voyages (arranged to make the best use of seasonal winds) to ferry merchants and settlers from Europe to colonies and trading settlements in distant lands.

Lumbering Portuguese carracks still sailed to the Spice Islands. But they were out of date. Merchants from richer trading nations – England, France and the Netherlands – sent huge East Indiamen to India, China and present-day Malaysia and Indonesia, to bring back all kinds of luxury goods. Fine cotton, tea, spices and dyestuffs came from India; China had silk, porcelain and jade for sale.

East Indiamen were rich prizes for pirates. One Dutch ship, which sank on its outward journey from Europe in 1724, had over three tonnes of silver (to pay for exotic goods) on board. So East Indiamen were armed with around 50 cannon and many smaller guns, as well.

MEN were kidnapped and forced to join the British Navy by the 'press gang', thugs paid to get recruits.

ON long voyages food quickly became stale. Sailors ate salted meat, hard, dry ship's biscuits, and wormy cheese.

BRITISH sailors had a daily ration of rum and water. By the late 18th century, they also had lime juice to stop scurvy.

ON BOARD ship discipline was harsh. Sailors could be locked in chains as a punishment or whipped with the 'cat of nine tails'.

The 'Jolly Roger', the skull-and-crossbones flag of pirate ships.

THE HEADQUARTERS of the Dutch East India Company in Bengal (present-day Bangladesh), early 18th century.

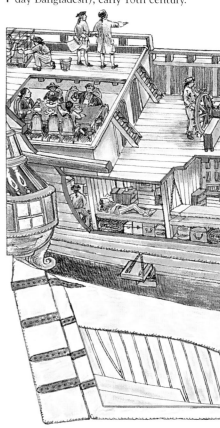

c1750

1760

1769

SLAVES having their hands fastened behind their backs in iron manacles (handcuffs), to stop them trying to escape. The first officially licensed European slave ships began sailing in 1537.

ILLUSTRATION from an 18th-century book showing how to fit as many captives as possible into a slave-ship. Many died in the terrible conditions before they reached the Caribbean.

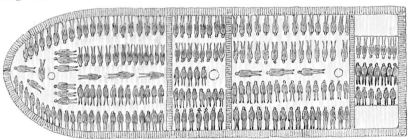

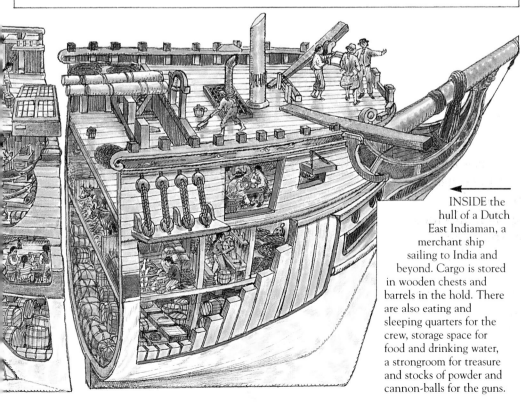

INSIDE the hull of a Dutch East Indiaman, a merchant ship sailing to India and beyond. Cargo is stored in wooden chests and barrels in the hold. There are also eating and sleeping quarters for the crew, storage space for food and drinking water, a strongroom for treasure and stocks of powder and cannon-balls for the guns.

1701 British 60-gun ship of the line, a ship strong enough to hold its place in a line of ships sailing into battle.

1710-1722 Danish timber ship. It has a huge hull for carrying bulky timber to England from Scandinavia. Pine was often used for shipbuilding, especially for interior fittings and for masts.

1728 The *Bucentaur*, a state barge built for the rulers of the city-state of Venice, in northern Italy. It was designed to look like a traditional war galley, but with sumptuous decoration. It was 35 metres long, 7 metres wide and needed 168 rowers.

c1750 English brigantine (small, two-masted vessel with square sails on both masts), used to ferry messages and lightweight goods along the coast.

1760 The *Hope*, a small cargo boat that traded around the Baltic Sea.

1769 Ship belonging to the Hudson's Bay Company, used to carry goods from Canada and North America across the Atlantic to Europe. These were much smaller than the huge cargo ships which carried goods from India and China to Europe during the same period. This was because the Atlantic crossing, though often very rough, could be made almost all year round. Ships to and from Asia had to wait for monsoon and trade winds to blow, so when they could sail merchants wanted them to carry as much as possible.

1768-1781

1775

1776

1789

MEN-OF-WAR

Hadley's quadrant was a navigational instrument invented in 1731. It enabled sailors to take sightings of the sun and stars while at sea. It was more accurate than the earlier astrolabe.

During the 18th century, powerful European nations (especially Britain and France) fought out their quarrels at sea. It was a time of epic naval battles, and of heroic commanders like Admiral Lord Nelson, who died in 1805 at the famous Battle of Trafalgar, off the coast of Spain.

European governments commissioned men-of-war, powerful battleships like Britain's HMS *Victory* or Spain's *Santissima Trinidad* for their navies. Naval battle tactics were brutally simple: sailing close together, these great ships advanced in a line towards the enemy. Each fleet intended to smash a hole with their cannon in the opposing navy's line, scatter their ships, surround them, then attack them individually.

After around 1750, European navies graded ships according to how many guns they could carry. A First Rate ship had 100 or more guns. (The *Victory* had 104, the *Santissima Trinidad* had 136.) At the bottom of the scale came a Fourth Rate ship, with 50 to 70 guns. Big, heavy ships like these were difficult to handle. (The *Victory* carried 32 different sails and had about 38 kilometres of rigging.) They needed expert officers and obedient crew.

lavatories

bow

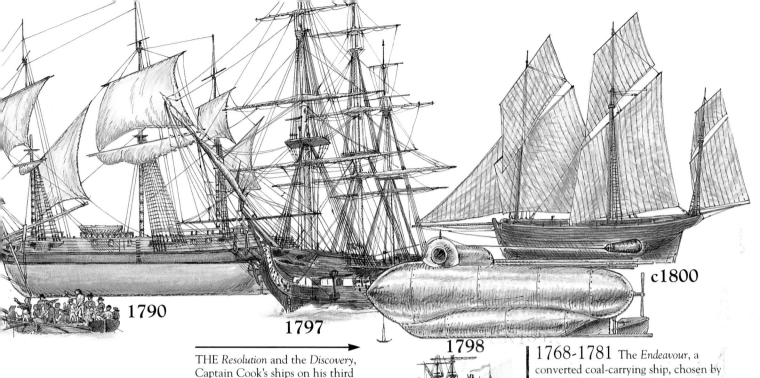

1790

1797

1798

c1800

THE *Resolution* and the *Discovery*, Captain Cook's ships on his third and final round-the-world voyage (1776-1780). Here, they are anchored off the north-west coast of Canada in 1778.

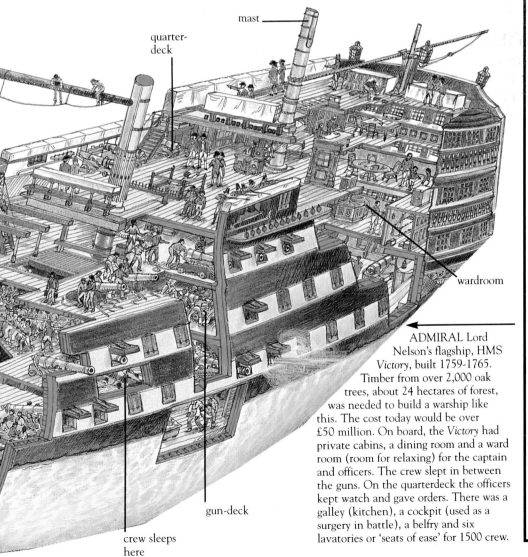

mast

quarter-deck

wardroom

ADMIRAL Lord Nelson's flagship, HMS *Victory*, built 1759-1765. Timber from over 2,000 oak trees, about 24 hectares of forest, was needed to build a warship like this. The cost today would be over £50 million. On board, the *Victory* had private cabins, a dining room and a ward room (room for relaxing) for the captain and officers. The crew slept in between the guns. On the quarterdeck the officers kept watch and gave orders. There was a galley (kitchen), a cockpit (used as a surgery in battle), a belfry and six lavatories or 'seats of ease' for 1500 crew.

gun-deck

crew sleeps here

1768-1781 The *Endeavour*, a converted coal-carrying ship, chosen by explorer Captain Cook for his voyage round the world. The cargo-hold was used for Cook's scientific equipment, and to store the plants and animals he collected on his voyage.

1775 The *Alliance*, a US Navy frigate (small, sail-powered warship with a single gun deck and fewer than 50 guns).

1776 The *Turtle* submarine, designed by American engineer David Bushnell. It was built of wood, like a barrel. Inside, it had tanks which could be pumped full of water to make it sink, or emptied to make it rise again. The *Turtle* was the first submarine to make an underwater attack on an enemy ship when it attacked a British naval vessel during the American War of Independence.

1789 HMS *Bounty*, scene of one of the most famous mutinies in British naval history.

1790 British navy frigate HMS *Pandora*, sent to capture the *Bounty* mutineers. On the homeward journey, the *Pandora* hit the Great Barrier Reef, off north-eastern Australia, and sank.

1797 US Navy frigate *Constitution*. It was still sailing in 1931.

1798 *Nautilus*, the first 'modern' submarine. It was made of iron and copper, 6.5 metres long and bullet shaped.

c1800 French lugger (fishing vessel). It had very large sails for the size of its hull, so it could sail fast. Perhaps this was why luggers were favourite pirate ships.

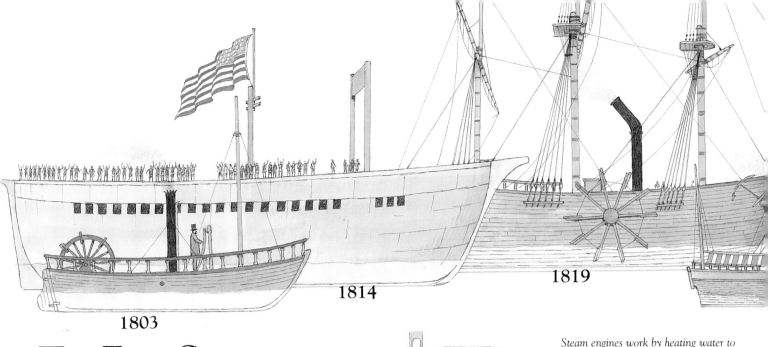

1803

1814

1819

The First Steamships

A screw propeller, the design fitted to most ships before c1860.

Scottish scientist James Watt built the first steam engine in 1765. Soon it was adapted for use in water as well as on land. In 1786 the first steam-powered boat was successfully tested on the Delaware River, USA, by its inventor, John Fitch. In 1790 he started to run a regular steam ferryboat service, but it was not a commercial success.

The first successful working steamboat, the *Charlotte Dundas*, was introduced in 1803. From then on, steam-powered boats became popular. They were especially suited to regular passenger and cargo trips along rivers or around the coast. Because they did not depend on the wind, they could keep to a published timetable. Stocks of wood or coal to fuel their engines could also be kept ready at ports along their route.

There was fierce competition between English and American sailors as to who could make the first transatlantic crossing in a ship powered by steam. In 1819 the *Savannah* (USA) did make the voyage, but, for much of its journey, it relied on sail. In 1838 the British *Sirius* made the first Atlantic crossing using steam power alone. There was competition, too, between steamships driven by side-mounted paddle-wheels and stern-mounted screws (propellers). Screws were more efficient, but were not widely used until after 1840.

Steam engines work by heating water to produce steam. The steam is trapped in pipes leading to metal cylinders. Each cylinder contains a sliding piston. As the steam flows into the cylinders, it pushes the pistons up the cylinders.

EACH piston is attached to a metal bar, a driving rod. As it is pushed along the cylinder, it moves the driving rod. At the same time, the driving rod turns another metal bar, the crankshaft. The crankshaft is connected to the ship's paddle-wheels or propellers which then move the water.

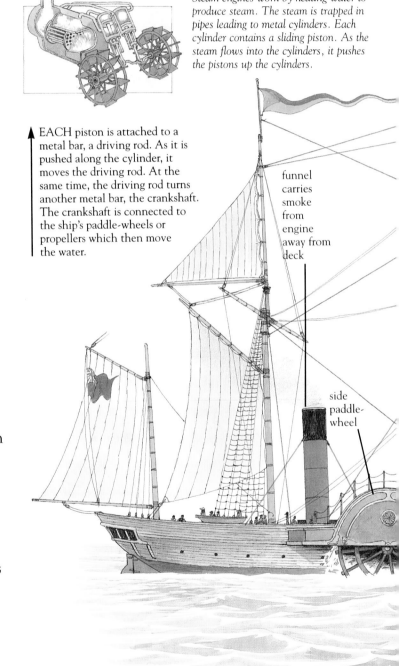

funnel carries smoke from engine away from deck

side paddle-wheel

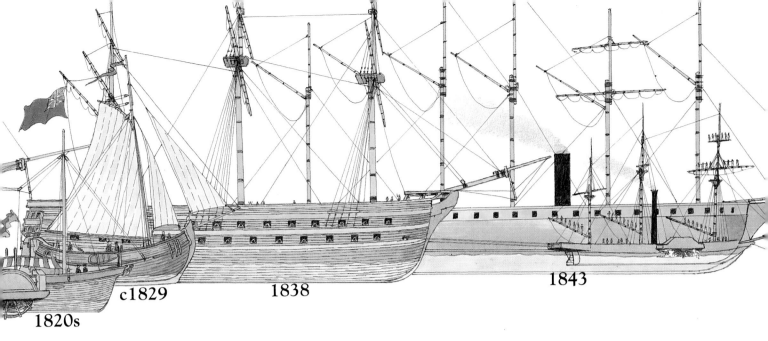

1820s

c1829

1838

1843

main mast and sails

FOR MANY years people could not agree whether propellers or paddle-wheels were more powerful. In 1845 a ships' tug-of-war was held to find out. Two similar-sized ships, the *Rattler* (propeller) and the *Alecto* (paddle-wheel) were tied together, stern to stern. Then both ships tried to sail straight ahead, in opposite directions, at full power. The *Rattler* won, quickly pulling the *Alecto* backwards.

ON ITS record-making voyage as the first steam-powered ship to cross the Atlantic, the *Sirius* almost ran out of fuel. The crew collected anything that would burn, including a mast and the ship's furniture.

1803 In Glasgow, in January, the paddle-steamer *Charlotte Dundas* was demonstrated for the first time. Then, in March, it towed two sailing boats 31 kilometres along the Forth and Clyde Canal against a strong wind.

1814 The *Fulton* (also known as the *Demologus*), was the world's first steam-powered warship. Its round, fortress-like design made it unsuitable for long journeys at sea; it was designed for harbour defence.

1819 The paddle-wheeled *Savannah* was the first steamship to cross the Atlantic. The journey (from Georgia, USA, to Liverpool, England) took 21 days.

1820s During the First Burma War the *Diana* became the first steam-powered warship to take an active part in a sea battle. A converted merchant ship, it was too small for guns, so was fitted with rockets instead.

c1829 Dutch schuyt, or sailing barge, used to carry goods along canals or in shallow estuaries and coastal waters.

1838 The sail-powered warship HMS *Hastings* being towed into harbour in Malta by the steam-powered tug *Rhadamanthes*.

1843 The SS *Great Britain*, designed by famous engineer, Isambard Kingdom Brunel, was the first passenger ship to be made mainly of iron. It was also the first to be driven by a propeller at the stern, rather than by a paddle-wheel on either side.

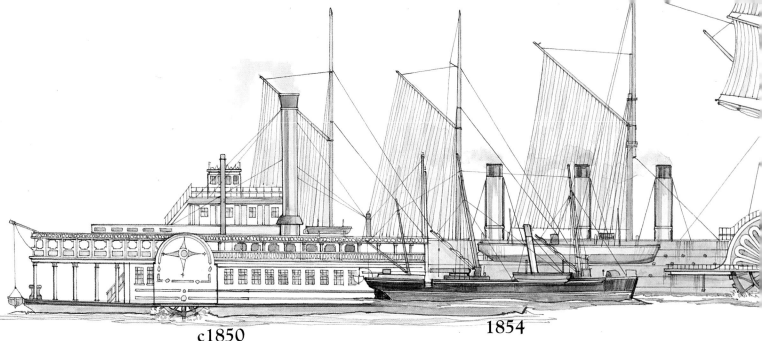

c1850

1854

IRONCLADS

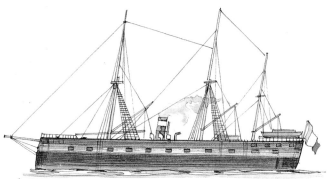

The river-steamer used by David Livingstone to explore the Zambezi River in central Africa in 1856.

For thousands of years, ships had been built of wood. But by the 1850s, new smelting techniques and manufacturing processes made it possible to build ships of iron. Iron was stronger than wood, and steam-powered engines, now widely used to propel larger and heavier vessels, increased the risk of fire on wooden ships. Iron was also better able to withstand direct hits from enemy guns. This became increasingly important as new guns were designed that could fire high-power exploding shells instead of cannon-balls.

The first metal ships were not made entirely of iron. They were ironclads, that is, wooden hulls encased in iron armour, or protected by a belt of iron around the waterline. Ironclads were widely used by both sides during the American Civil War (1861-1865). In March 1862 there was a famous 'dog-fight' between two of them – the *Merrimack* and the *Monitor*. Protected by their iron casing neither could sink the other.

The first completely iron-hulled ships were the French *Gloire* (1859) and the British *Warrior* (1860). They had steam engines, but masts and sails too, just in case the engines broke down.

FRENCH ironclad battleship, the *Gloire*, built 1859. It carried 36 powerful cannon, and was fitted with both steam engines and sails.

STEAM-POWERED, ironclad gunships belonging to the Union (northern) side, in action on the Mississippi River in 1862, during the American Civil War.

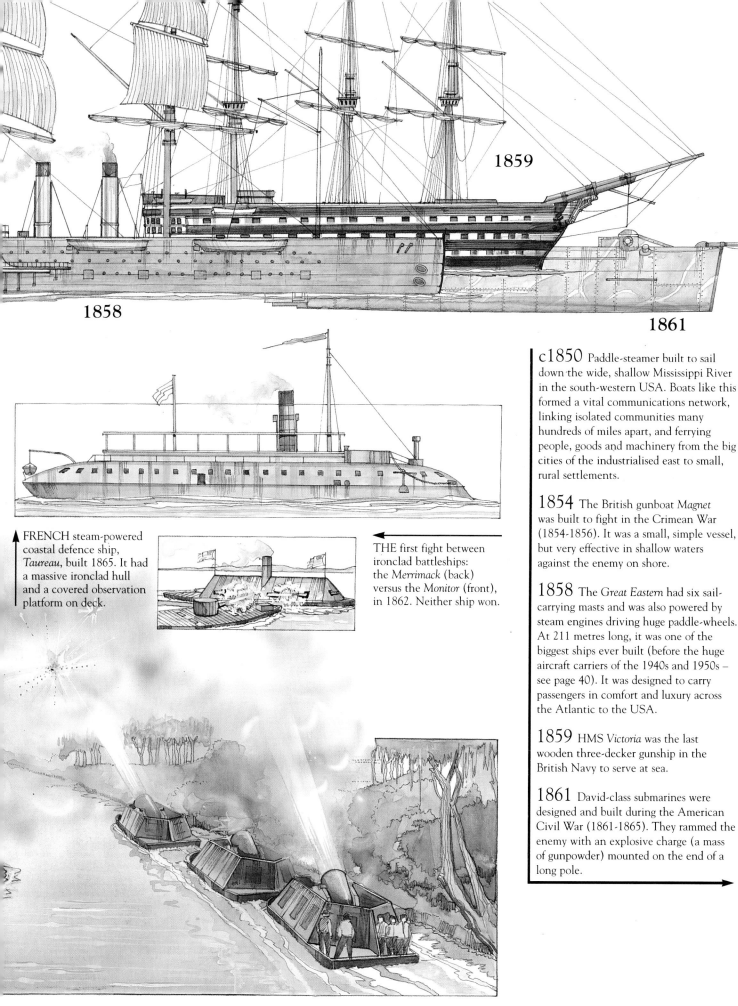

1859

1858

1861

FRENCH steam-powered coastal defence ship, *Taureau*, built 1865. It had a massive ironclad hull and a covered observation platform on deck.

THE first fight between ironclad battleships: the *Merrimack* (back) versus the *Monitor* (front), in 1862. Neither ship won.

c1850 Paddle-steamer built to sail down the wide, shallow Mississippi River in the south-western USA. Boats like this formed a vital communications network, linking isolated communities many hundreds of miles apart, and ferrying people, goods and machinery from the big cities of the industrialised east to small, rural settlements.

1854 The British gunboat *Magnet* was built to fight in the Crimean War (1854-1856). It was a small, simple vessel, but very effective in shallow waters against the enemy on shore.

1858 The *Great Eastern* had six sail-carrying masts and was also powered by steam engines driving huge paddle-wheels. At 211 metres long, it was one of the biggest ships ever built (before the huge aircraft carriers of the 1940s and 1950s – see page 40). It was designed to carry passengers in comfort and luxury across the Atlantic to the USA.

1859 HMS *Victoria* was the last wooden three-decker gunship in the British Navy to serve at sea.

1861 David-class submarines were designed and built during the American Civil War (1861-1865). They rammed the enemy with an explosive charge (a mass of gunpowder) mounted on the end of a long pole.

1876

1874

1876

TRADITION AND EXPERIMENT

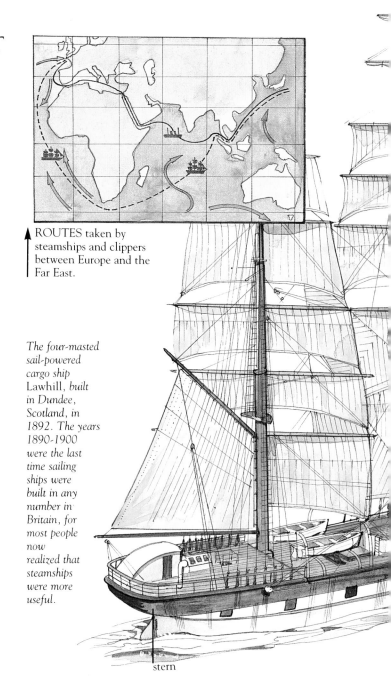

The passenger ship Vicksburg, built in 1872 to sail between Liverpool and Canada.

Steam ships could only carry a limited amount of coal, and refuelling stops were always necessary on long-distance voyages. So clippers, big, ocean-going sailing ships, were still used on many international routes. With a following wind, clippers could still sail much faster than steamships. In 1866, two clippers completed the 25,600-kilometre journey from China to London in 99 days. One hundred years earlier the journey had taken eight months.

Steamships had started to replace clippers by the late 1850s, although clippers were still used to bring tea from China and wool from Australia until almost the end of the century. After the Suez Canal opened in 1869, steamships had a much shorter journey to and from India and the Far East. But clippers still had to sail around Africa as there was not enough wind for them along the Suez Canal. Coaling stations were established all round the world, so fuelling problems were overcome. And steamships, with their very powerful engines, could carry far more cargo than clippers.

The end of the 19th century also saw many experiments in ship design. Some, like the new naval submarines, were highly effective. Others, like bulging French battleships and the round ships built to guard Russian harbours, were not.

ROUTES taken by steamships and clippers between Europe and the Far East.

The four-masted sail-powered cargo ship Lawhill, built in Dundee, Scotland, in 1892. The years 1890-1900 were the last time sailing ships were built in any number in Britain, for most people now realized that steamships were more useful.

stern

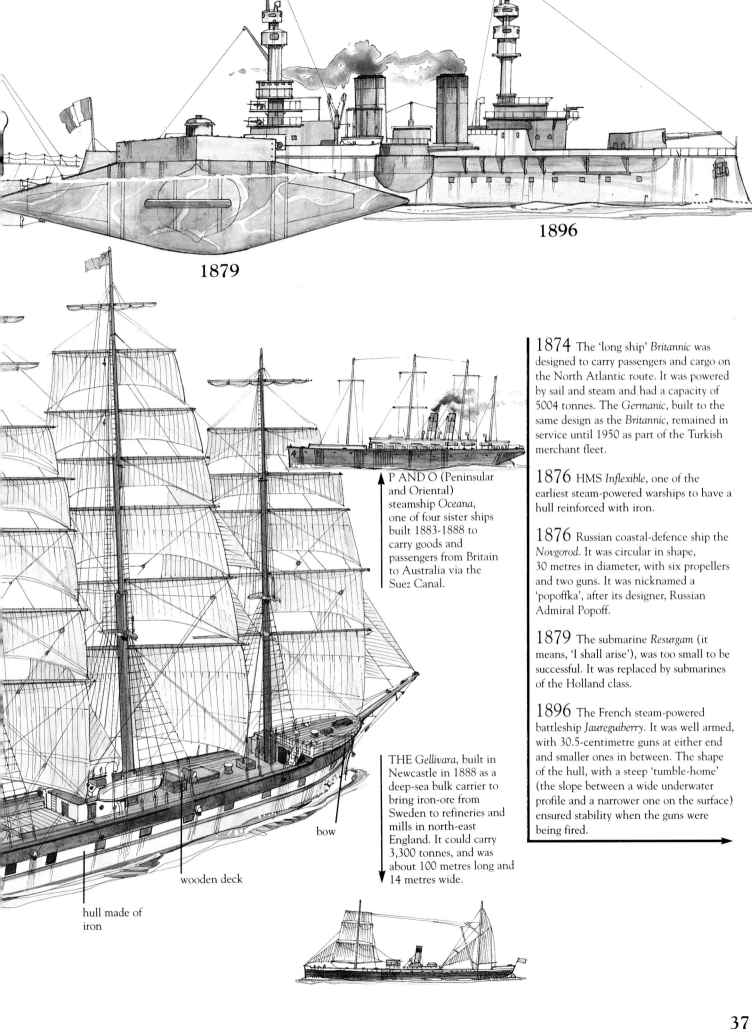

1896

1879

P AND O (Peninsular and Oriental) steamship *Oceana*, one of four sister ships built 1883-1888 to carry goods and passengers from Britain to Australia via the Suez Canal.

THE *Gellivara*, built in Newcastle in 1888 as a deep-sea bulk carrier to bring iron-ore from Sweden to refineries and mills in north-east England. It could carry 3,300 tonnes, and was about 100 metres long and 14 metres wide.

bow

wooden deck

hull made of iron

1874 The 'long ship' *Britannic* was designed to carry passengers and cargo on the North Atlantic route. It was powered by sail and steam and had a capacity of 5004 tonnes. The *Germanic*, built to the same design as the *Britannic*, remained in service until 1950 as part of the Turkish merchant fleet.

1876 HMS *Inflexible*, one of the earliest steam-powered warships to have a hull reinforced with iron.

1876 Russian coastal-defence ship the *Novgorod*. It was circular in shape, 30 metres in diameter, with six propellers and two guns. It was nicknamed a 'popoffka', after its designer, Russian Admiral Popoff.

1879 The submarine *Resurgam* (it means, 'I shall arise'), was too small to be successful. It was replaced by submarines of the Holland class.

1896 The French steam-powered battleship *Jaureguiberry*. It was well armed, with 30.5-centimetre guns at either end and smaller ones in between. The shape of the hull, with a steep 'tumble-home' (the slope between a wide underwater profile and a narrower one on the surface) ensured stability when the guns were being fired.

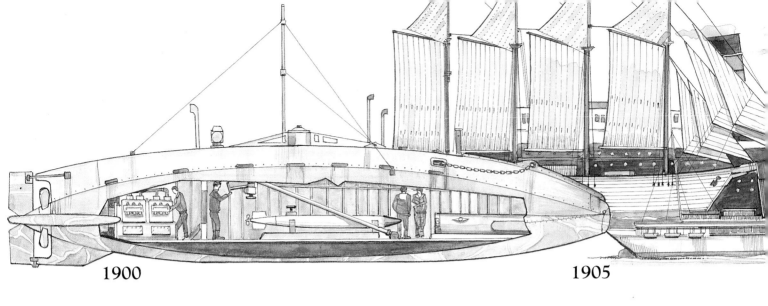

1900

1905

LINERS AND BATTLESHIPS

Metal shells fired from battleships had explosive tips and were filled with metal balls.

The early years of the 20th century were the great age of passenger travel by sea. Machine-assisted shipbuilding techniques and new steam turbine engines (invented in 1894) meant that huge passenger liners could be designed to be fast, elegant and powerful. The fastest transatlantic liner, RMS *Mauretania*, could make the journey in only four days.

Once passengers were aboard a big liner, it was sometimes hard for them to remember that they were at sea. Liners were designed to look like floating hotels, or even small towns. The largest carried around 2,000 passengers, and provided comfortable facilities for them all. There were ballrooms, libraries, gymnasiums, swimming pools, concert halls and theatres, as well as private cabin accommodation, and rooms where all the staff worked. The *Titanic* was the largest liner ever built, and, at 52,250 tonnes, the world's biggest ship in 1912. Its first-class dining-room was almost 35 metres long.

Early 20th-century battleships were also very, very big. Like ocean liners, the iron-hulled British *Dreadnought* (17,900 tonnes) was powered by fast steam turbine engines, and could travel at 21 knots. It was about 152 metres long and 24 metres wide. It had 24 massive guns, which took only 30 seconds to load, aim and fire.

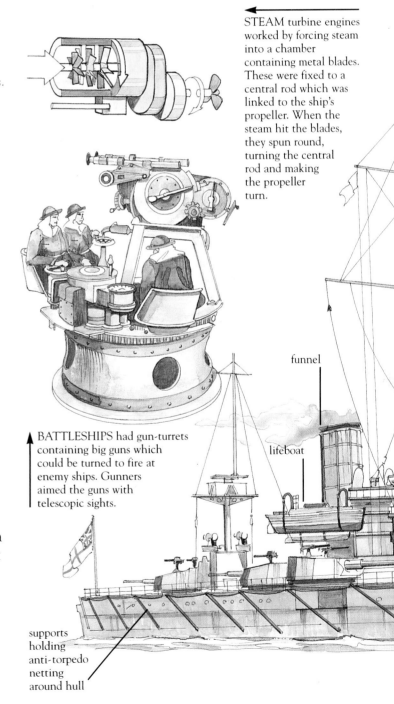

STEAM turbine engines worked by forcing steam into a chamber containing metal blades. These were fixed to a central rod which was linked to the ship's propeller. When the steam hit the blades, they spun round, turning the central rod and making the propeller turn.

BATTLESHIPS had gun-turrets containing big guns which could be turned to fire at enemy ships. Gunners aimed the guns with telescopic sights.

funnel

lifeboat

supports holding anti-torpedo netting around hull

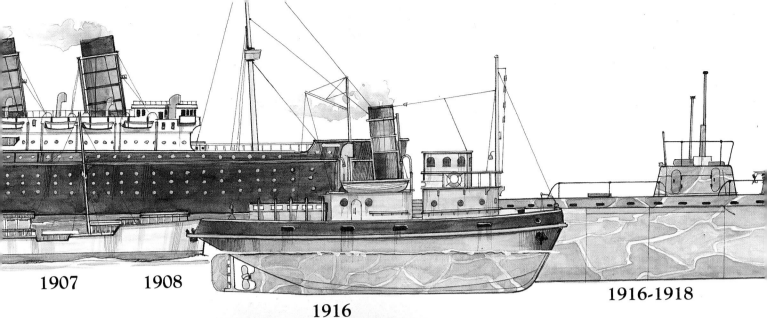

1907   1908

1916

1916-1918

THE *Titanic* had watertight bulkheads (inner walls), dividing the hull into 15 separate parts. If one filled with water, the rest would stay dry. This did not happen when the *Titanic* hit an iceberg on its first voyage in 1912. It sank and 1522 people died.

1900 Holland-class submarines, made in America, were the first submersible craft with two effective engines: a petrol motor for surface use and an electric one for use under the sea.

1905 Pacuare banana boats were designed to carry fruit from the Caribbean to Europe. They could carry a few passengers, for a leisurely cruise, as well.

1907 RMS *Mauretania* was, at this time, the biggest liner ever built. It could carry 2,165 passengers on the transatlantic route from Europe to the USA. Between 1909-1929 the *Mauretania* held the 'Blue Riband', for the fastest Atlantic crossing by a passenger liner: four days.

1908 Sail-powered ships were still in use in the early 20th century. This schooner (a small, fast sailing vessel), the *Bertha L Downes*, carried coal along the New England coast of North America.

bridge for captain and navigators

THE battleship HMS *Dreadnought*, launched in 1906, was the pride of Britain's battle fleet. It was iron-hulled, steam-powered and carried 5 separate gun-turrets, to provide 'all round' gunfire.

THE *Titanic* did not have enough lifeboats for all the passengers. After the disaster international laws were changed and all ships must have enough lifeboats for everyone on board.

1916 Tugs like this helped move warships and liners in confined spaces: channels, harbours and canals. They were driven by steam or diesel engines. A really large ship might need four or six tugs to guide it safely into port.

1916-1918 German U-boat ('*Unterseeboot*': undersea-boat) used to lay mines to destroy British shipping during the First World War. U-boats came close to crippling the British fleet.

gun-turret

iron hull   anchors

1934   1939-1945

WAR AND PEACE

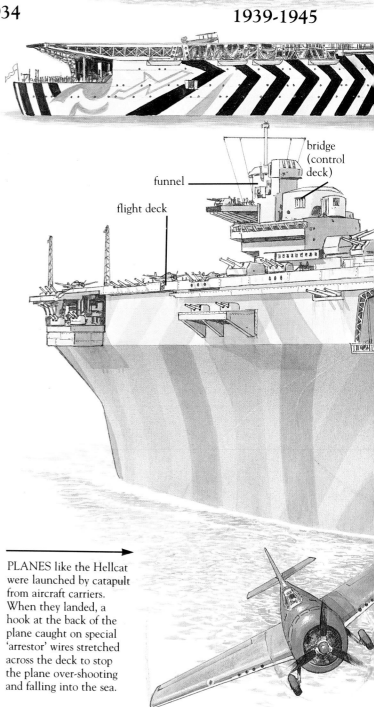

Hellcat fighter plane, carried by American aircraft carriers during the Second World War.

Ships from many nations played an important part in the Second World War. Old battleships and their crews performed heroically, and two new Japanese battleships, the *Yamato* and the *Musashi* (both 1940), were the biggest ever built. But new types of ship, aircraft carriers and submarines, showed that big guns were not always necessary, guided missiles and planes could attack instead.

Submarines were vital. They destroyed enemy ships and laid mines in enemy waters. German U-boats almost managed to stop the British merchant fleet delivering essential supplies of food and fuel. Merchant ships vulnerable to submarine attack travelled in convoys, escorted by frigates and destroyers, constantly on guard.

Aircraft carriers transformed warfare, at sea and on land. They could bring helicopters and planes within reach of formerly inaccessible targets. They could provide an airfield almost anywhere it was needed and then take it away if it was threatened with attack.

Before and after the war, ships were still used for pleasure. Big liners remained in service, as yet there were no jumbo jets.

bridge (control deck)

funnel

flight deck

PLANES like the Hellcat were launched by catapult from aircraft carriers. When they landed, a hook at the back of the plane caught on special 'arrestor' wires stretched across the deck to stop the plane over-shooting and falling into the sea.

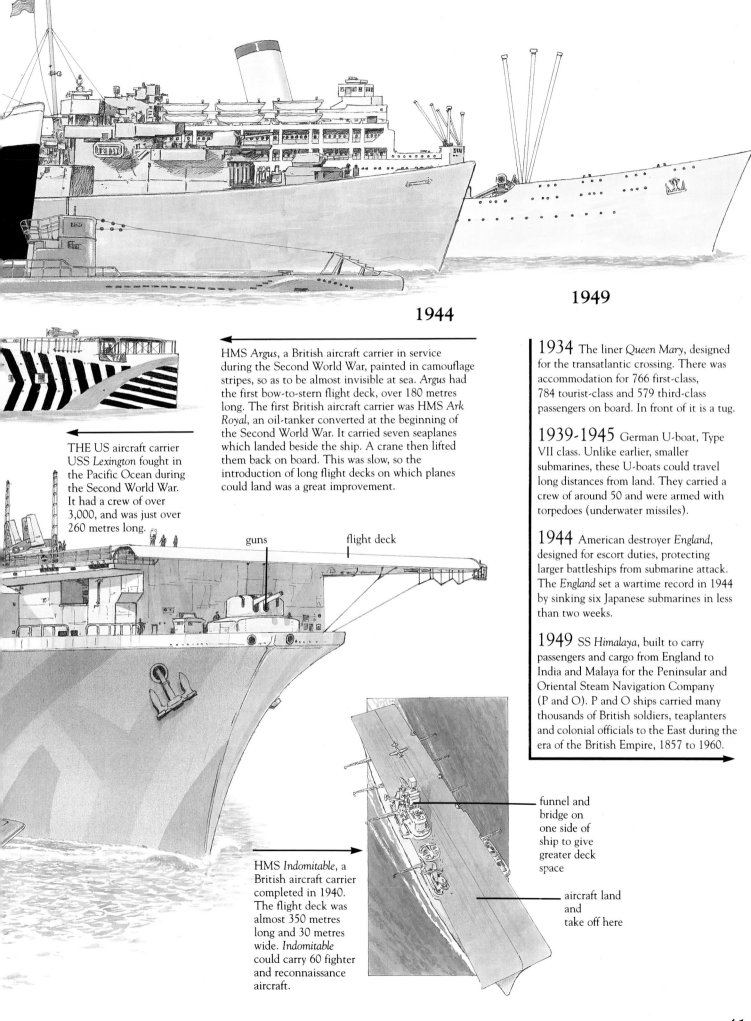

1944

1949

HMS *Argus*, a British aircraft carrier in service during the Second World War, painted in camouflage stripes, so as to be almost invisible at sea. *Argus* had the first bow-to-stern flight deck, over 180 metres long. The first British aircraft carrier was HMS *Ark Royal*, an oil-tanker converted at the beginning of the Second World War. It carried seven seaplanes which landed beside the ship. A crane then lifted them back on board. This was slow, so the introduction of long flight decks on which planes could land was a great improvement.

THE US aircraft carrier USS *Lexington* fought in the Pacific Ocean during the Second World War. It had a crew of over 3,000, and was just over 260 metres long.

guns

flight deck

1934 The liner *Queen Mary*, designed for the transatlantic crossing. There was accommodation for 766 first-class, 784 tourist-class and 579 third-class passengers on board. In front of it is a tug.

1939-1945 German U-boat, Type VII class. Unlike earlier, smaller submarines, these U-boats could travel long distances from land. They carried a crew of around 50 and were armed with torpedoes (underwater missiles).

1944 American destroyer *England*, designed for escort duties, protecting larger battleships from submarine attack. The *England* set a wartime record in 1944 by sinking six Japanese submarines in less than two weeks.

1949 SS *Himalaya*, built to carry passengers and cargo from England to India and Malaya for the Peninsular and Oriental Steam Navigation Company (P and O). P and O ships carried many thousands of British soldiers, teaplanters and colonial officials to the East during the era of the British Empire, 1857 to 1960.

funnel and bridge on one side of ship to give greater deck space

aircraft land and take off here

HMS *Indomitable*, a British aircraft carrier completed in 1940. The flight deck was almost 350 metres long and 30 metres wide. *Indomitable* could carry 60 fighter and reconnaissance aircraft.

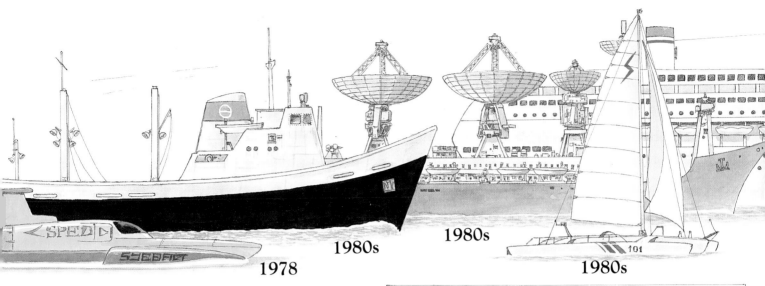

1978 **1980s** **1980s** **1980s**

Ships for Today

Ro-ro (roll-on, roll-off) ferry. Vehicles drive on and off through huge bow and stern 'visors' (sections of the hull that lift up).

People often say that the world is becoming a smaller place. What do they mean? Sometimes they are talking about instant mass-communications: round-the-globe telephone, television and computer links. But often they are talking about travel. Since the 1960s, quick, fast, safe air transport has been available to almost anywhere in the world, at a price many ordinary people can afford. Cheap and quick air transport is also available on many cargo routes. So what use are ships and boats today?

Boats are still used for short trips – when the speed of an aircraft does not really count, or where there is nowhere suitable for a plane to land. And boats are increasingly used for fun: from the stateliest luxury yacht to the simplest windsurfing board. Cruises are popular holidays. Power-boat racing and small-boat sailing are also very popular outdoor sports.

Ships have been designed for special activities: radio monitoring, scientific research or saving lives. But, perhaps surprisingly, ships are still the best and cheapest means of transporting large loads across water – just as they were thousands of years ago.

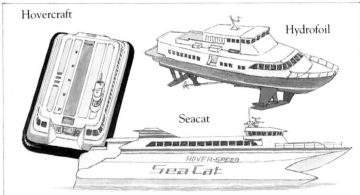

Hovercraft Hydrofoil Seacat

HOVERCRAFT skim over the surface of the water on a cushion of air trapped inside their rubber skirts. Strictly speaking, hovercraft are not ships, because their hulls are not in the water. Hydrofoils have hulls, but, at speed, they rise above the water on curved metal 'foils' attached to the hull, which act rather like water-skis. Seacats (sea catamarans) have specially-designed twin hulls, which act rather like foils.

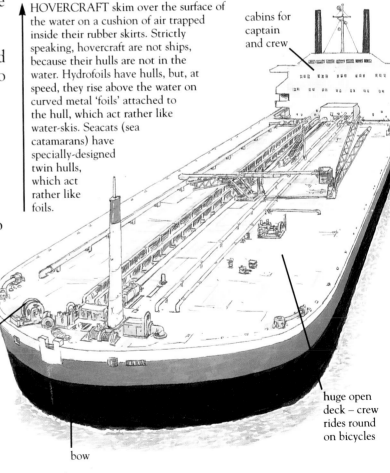

cabins for captain and crew

winches to wind ropes used to tie tanker to dock

huge open deck – crew rides round on bicycles

bow

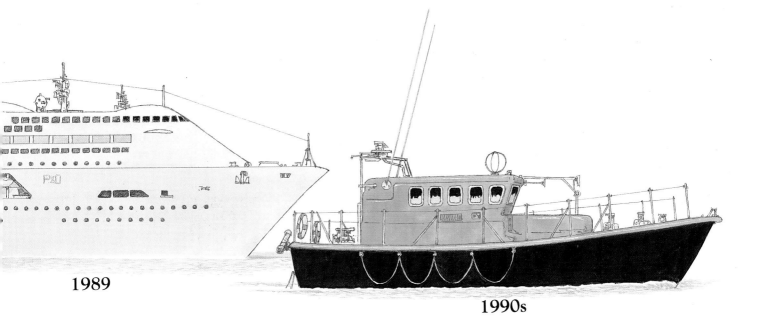

1989

1990s

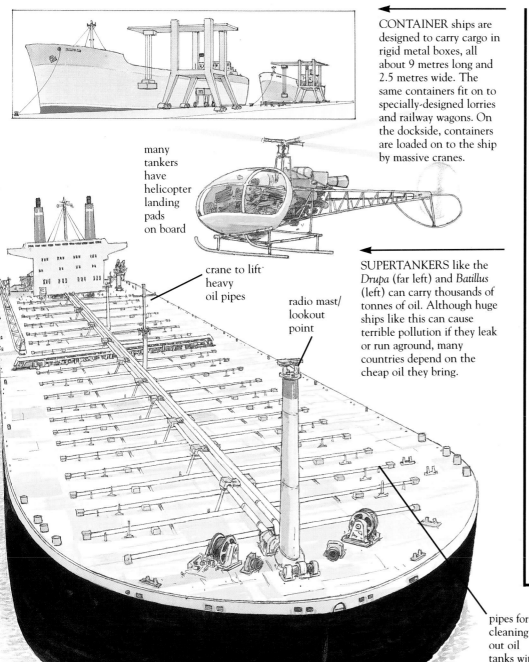

CONTAINER ships are designed to carry cargo in rigid metal boxes, all about 9 metres long and 2.5 metres wide. The same containers fit on to specially-designed lorries and railway wagons. On the dockside, containers are loaded on to the ship by massive cranes.

many tankers have helicopter landing pads on board

crane to lift heavy oil pipes

radio mast/ lookout point

SUPERTANKERS like the *Drupa* (far left) and *Batillus* (left) can carry thousands of tonnes of oil. Although huge ships like this can cause terrible pollution if they leak or run aground, many countries depend on the cheap oil they bring.

pipes for cleaning out oil tanks with seawater

1978 *Spirit of Australia*, a speedboat propelled by jet engines. It set a world water-speed record of 514 km/h.

1980s Factory-ship trawler, used to catch fish, gut and freeze them (at -28°C), while at sea. Some factory ships also employ skilled workers to trim and fillet the fish, ready for sale in shops. Trawlers like this operate in North Altantic waters. They can stay at sea for several weeks at a time. Some scientists think that they lead to over-fishing, and that there might soon be no more fish left.

1980s The Soviet communications ship *Kosmonaut Yuri Gagarin* carried important, and secret, scientific research equipment, for use in the USSR's space programme.

1980s Trimarans with light fibre-glass hulls and strong carbon-fibre masts, won most of the major long-distance races for sailing yachts.

1989 SS *Crown Princess*, a luxury cruise ship, or 'floating hotel'. Holidaymakers travel in great comfort on ships like these, calling in at places of interest on land during the day, but returning on board to sleep in their cabins at night.

1990s Tyne-class lifeboat used by the Royal National Lifeboat Institution to save sailors from wrecked ships all round the British coast. It has a light steel hull, powerful diesel engines and flotation chambers packed with air-filled foam. It carries a crew of six.

43

Ship facts

The funeral barge of Pharaoh Khufu is the world's oldest surviving boat. It was buried with him in his tomb, around 2500 BC, and was designed to ferry his soul to the next world. Because of its religious importance, Khufu's barge was made of valuable, sweet-smelling cedar wood. The dry air of the tomb had preserved it.

The Battle of Salamis, fought in 480 BC between Greek and Persian (Iranian) fleets, changed the course of history. The Greeks won, and halted a Persian invasion. If the Greeks had lost, the Persians would have taken over their land. Many great Greek temples, statues, carvings and other beautiful objects that have inspired European artists for hundreds of years, and which people still admire today, would never have been made.

The Battle of Actium in 31 BC also decided the fate of empires – and led to a personal tragedy. At Actium, the Roman navy defeated a battle fleet belonging to Queen Cleopatra of Egypt and her lover, rebel Roman general Mark Antony. The Romans won, and Cleopatra killed herself rather than face capture by Rome.

There are legends that people from the west coast of South America migrated to remote Pacific islands around AD 1100, sailing across the Pacific Ocean on rafts of balsa-wood, a very light wood. In 1947, the explorer Thor Heyerdahl built a copy of a traditional South American balsa raft (which he named the *Kon-Tiki*) and set sail. He arrived safely on a Pacific island, proving that such a journey could be made.

The Portuguese caravel *Vittoria* became the first ship to sail right round the world, in 1519-1521. Its captain was the explorer Ferdinand Magellan, but he did not live to complete the voyage. He was killed in the Pacific in 1520. After Magellan's death, the *Vittoria* was sailed home by one of his officers, Juan Sebastian del Cano.

The Battle of Lepanto, fought between Italian and Turkish fleets off the coast of Greece in 1571, was the last major battle in Europe in which the ships were powered by oars. It was the end of a tradition over 2000 years old.

The world's first yacht club was founded over 250 years ago, in 1720 at Cork, in Ireland.

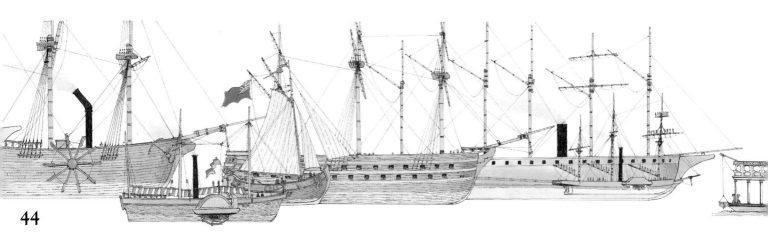

In October 1872, the cargo ship *Marie Celeste* left New York Harbor with ten people on board. A month later, it was found drifting and abandoned in the Atlantic Ocean. The ship was undamaged, but the passengers and crew seemed to have left in a great hurry. No trace of them has ever been found.

At Tsushima, in 1905, the Japanese fleet heavily defeated the Russian fleet. This was the last sea battle to be fought by ships alone.

The last big battle in traditional naval style, between two fleets of enemy battleships, was the Battle of Jutland between Britain and Germany in 1916, in the North Sea off Denmark.

The first specially-designed aircraft carriers were launched in 1923, the British *Hermes* and the Japanese *Hosho*.

The first nuclear-powered submarine, the USS *Nautilus*, was completed in 1955.

The first hovercraft passenger service started in 1968, using British SRN-4 hovercraft for the Channel crossing to France.

The American attack-carrier USS *Enterprise* (completed 1961) was the first nuclear-powered warship and the largest warship ever built. (The American aircraft carrier *Nimitz* is very nearly as big.) It is 341.3 metres long and 75,700 tonnes. It can carry about 100 planes, and can also fire supersonic anti-aircraft missiles.

Guided-missile destroyers of the British Navy's 'county' class (built 1963-1970) are completely washable. They have been designed so that every part of the ship can be washed down and decontaminated if they ever become polluted by radioactive fallout in a nuclear war.

The Falklands War of 1982, between Britain and Argentina, was the first war to be fought largely by missiles fired from ships. French-made Exocet missiles proved to have deadly destructive power.

Supertanker *Exxon Valdez* ran aground off Alaska in 1988, flooding 1,930 kilometres of remote coastline with oil, and killing local wildlife. It was the worst ecological disaster caused by a ship.

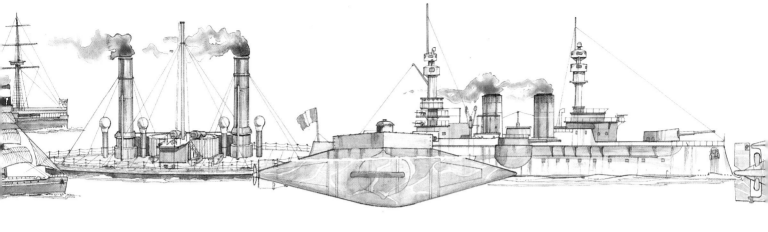

GLOSSARY

Anchor Heavy weight, often shaped like a large arrow, fixed to the end of long rope or chain, to moor a ship to the sea bottom.

Astrolabe An instrument used by sailors to find out a ship's latitude: how far north or south of the equator it was. The astrolabe measured the height of the sun or, at night, the Pole Star, above the horizon.

Bow The front end of a ship or boat.

Broadside A row of cannon all pointing in the same direction (through holes cut in the side of a ship). When fired all at once, they were a formidable weapon.

Buoyancy The ability to float. Bouyancy is determined by density, that is, the mass (weight) of an object in relation to its volume. Something that is large and not very dense will float better than a small, very dense object.

Caravel A small deck above the main bow or stern decks.

Castle A small, light sailing ship with three or four masts and lateen sails. Sailed by Portuguese and Spanish explorers in the 15th and 16th centuries.

Carrack A large merchant ship, developed in Europe around 1400. It combined northern European square sails with southern European lateen ones.

Carvel A method of building ships using planks fitted edge-to-edge to make the hull.

Catamaran Ship or boat with two hulls.

Clinker A method of building ships using overlapping planks to make the hull.

Destroyer A small, 20th-century fighting ship designed to escort larger battleships and to hunt and destroy enemy submarines.

Draught (sometimes spelled draft) The amount of water a ship needs to sail without running aground.

Galleon A large 16th-century ship, used for trade and war. Similar to a carrack, but with lower castles at bow and stern.

Galley A large warship powered by oars as well as by big, square sails.

Hull The 'body' of a ship; the part that sits in the water.

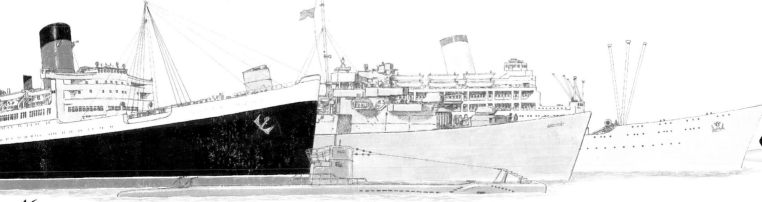

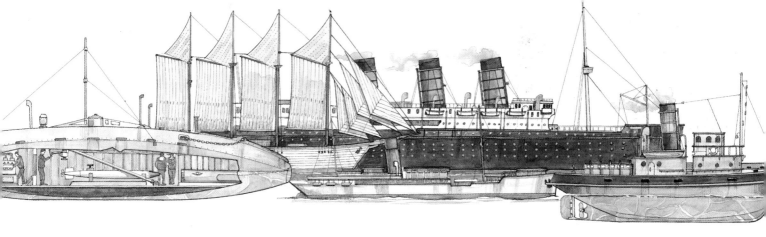

Keel The bottom part of the hull.

Lateen A triangular sail, often used on ships in the Mediterranean Sea and in the Persian Gulf.

Log In seagoing terms, a written diary of a voyage, kept by the captain or the ship's officers.

Mainsail The biggest sail on a wind-powered sailing ship.

Mizzen The mast behind the main mast.

Monsoon A wind in India and southern Asia which blows from the south-west in the summer and the north-east in the winter.

Navigation Steering an accurate course at sea.

Outrigger A wooden framework fitted to the side of a boat (usually a canoe) to give extra space for rowers. It also provided extra stability.

Port Left-hand side of the ship, when facing towards the bow (front).

Ribs The wooden framework around which a ship's hull was built.

Rigging Ropes holding the sails and the masts in position.

Rudder Large paddle fixed to a ship's stern and used to steer it. Invented in China before AD 1000; used in Europe from around 1300.

Scurvy A disease caused by a shortage of vitamin C. It was common among sailors on long voyages who went for weeks without any fresh food. Captain Cook solved the problem by ensuring that his crews had lime juice regularly. Citrus fruit, like limes, are rich in vitamin C.

Sea-chest Wooden chest in which sailors stored their belongings.

Sewn Term applied to boats that have their planks lashed together with ropes or twine.

Starboard The right-hand side of a ship, when facing towards the bow (front).

Stern Back end of a ship or boat.

Trade wind A wind that blows constantly towards the equator.

Turbine An efficient engine, which uses steam to create a powerful thrust to drive a ship through the water.

U-boat German submarine, used in the First and Second World Wars.

INDEX